look wider

look wider

Published by Girlguiding UK
17–19 Buckingham Palace Road
London
SW1W 0PT
Email chq@girlguiding.org.uk
Website www.girlguiding.org.uk

Girlguiding UK is an operating name of The Guide Association.
Registered charity number 306016. Incorporated by Royal Charter.

© The Guide Association 1994-2007

ISBN 978 0 85260 166 2
Printed by Paul Green Printing Ltd

Girlguiding UK Trading Service ordering code 6021

Look Wider working group Jean Bell, Judy Edwards, Jo Haddrick, Sam Harrold, Morag Nimmo, Katie Pitkin and Susanne Ranson

The Senior Section members who appear in this personal organiser are from 18th Croydon Rangers and STAR Rangers (Deptford).

Writer Michèle Roche
Photographer (Senior Section members) Diana Aynaci
Stylist Soraya
Senior Project Editor Alice Forbes
Project Editor Clare Jeater, Rebecca Saraceno
Editor Annabelle Mundy
Special Project Designer David Jones
Studio Janie Barton and Alexandra Valy

Readers are reminded that during the life span of this publication there may be changes to:
○ Girlguiding UK's policy
○ practice or requirements by governing bodies or other organisations
○ legal requirements
which will affect the accuracy of the information contained within these pages.

Contents

Personal details	2
Senior Section info	4
What is Look Wider?	7
Making Look Wider work for me	9
My guiding values	11
Helping hands	13
My long-term goals	14
Choosing a challenge	16
Personal plans	18
Understanding my strengths	19
My communication style	21
What kind of communicator am I?	23
Active planning	25
Am I making progress?	27
Answering my challenges	28
Getting going	29
Create your dreams	30
Health and happiness	34
Action for others	38
Get out and have fun	42
World vision	46
Right moves for me	50
You are who you are	54
Lead the way	58
Take your chance	62
Take on a new role	64
Group dynamics	67
Fun overseas	70
More strings to your bow	71
Camps, holidays and overnight events	76

LOOK WIDER LOOK WIDER **LOOK WIDER** LOOK WIDER **LOOK WIDER** LOOK WIDER

Emergency info
about me

Emergency contact

| Name |
| Address |
| |
| |
| Postcode |
| ☎ |
| Mobile |
| Email |

Medical info

| Doctor |
| ☎ |
| Medical details |
| |
| Allergies |
| |
| Hospital consultant |
| Hospital |
| Hospital number |

This Look Wider organiser belongs to

Name

Address

Postcode

☎

Mobile

Email

Date of birth

NI number

Passport number

Driving licence number

Bank details

Credit card ☎

Dentist

Name

☎

Optician

Name

☎

LOOK WIDER **FOR** CONTACTS **FOR** LIFE

Senior Section info

I am a member of the _____ Senior Section Group.

We meet at _____

on _____ (day/evening).

My Senior Section Leader

| Name |
| Address |
| |
| Postcode |
| ☎ |
| Mobile |
| Email |

My District Commissioner

| Name |
| Address |
| |
| Postcode |
| ☎ |
| Mobile |
| Email |

LOOK WIDER **FOR** CONTACTS **FOR** LIFE

Senior Section
Group details

- Name
- Team role
- Address

- Postcode
- ☎
- Mobile
- Email

- Name
- Team role
- Address

- Postcode
- ☎
- Mobile
- Email

LOOK WIDER **FOR** CONTACTS **FOR** LIFE

| Name |
| Team role |
| Address |
| |
| Postcode |
| ☎ |
| Mobile |
| Email |

| Name |
| Team role |
| Address |
| |
| Postcode |
| ☎ |
| Mobile |
| Email |

Girlguiding UK contacts
CHQ
Girlguiding UK, 17–19 Buckingham Palace Road,
London SW1W 0PT ☎ 020 7834 6242 Fax 020 7828 8317
Email chq@girlguiding.org.uk Website www.girlguiding.org.uk

Guiding Essentials
Girlguiding UK Trading Service, Atlantic Street, Broadheath,
Altrincham, Cheshire, WA14 5EQ
☎ 0161 941 2237 Fax 0161 941 6326
Email tradings@girlguiding.org.uk
Website www.girlguiding.org.uk/shop

What is Look Wider?

Look Wider is Girlguiding UK's personal development programme for young women aged 14 to 25. It will help you...
to do all you can do, to be all you can be.

look wider

Look Wider is all about giving you a framework so you can identify your goals – and realise them. Along the way you'll have the opportunity to develop skills that will not just help you now, but that'll help you throughout life.

Look Wider is a flexible programme organised under eight key areas called Octants, each with a range of challenges. There's no preset model: you can work on your own, with someone else or in a team. You can work through the programme in a structured way or adopt an informal approach.

LOOK WIDER FOR MORE INFO ON PAGES 5–13 OF THE MAIN FILE.

Using my Look Wider organiser

This organiser has got all you need to get started on Look Wider. There is also a main *Look Wider* file containing lots more information.

> Use your Look Wider organiser to monitor your progress and record your achievements as you work on your challenges. You'll be able to build up a picture of what you're aiming for in terms of your personal development as well as the steps you're going to take to get there. Keep updating it, so you accommodate new goals. And keep it safe so you can always refer to it later.

Making
Look Wider work for me

You have a huge choice of where to start. For each Octant there are about 50 challenges suggested in the main file. To get a taste of what it's all about, you'll find six challenges for each Octant on pages 30–58 of this organiser.

How you choose your challenge depends on you. You can dip in to the suggested challenges and see what takes your fancy. Or you can work out what you want to achieve, then decide which challenges will help you reach your goals. On pages 14–27 are some personal development planning ideas to help you work out realistic goals.

- Leadership
- Creativity
- Fit for life
- Community action
- Out of doors
- International
- Independent living
- Personal values

The choice is yours! If you can think of a challenge, you can do it! All that matters is that what you do is a challenge to you.

LOOK **WIDER** FOR **MORE** INFO **ON** PAGES **52–70** OF **THE MAIN FILE**.

Don't be phased...

Each Octant has three Phases:
- Phase 1 – Starting something.
- Phase 2 – Building on it.
- Phase 3 – Taking things further.

Each Phase represents a different level of development, from trying something new to passing on your skills to others.

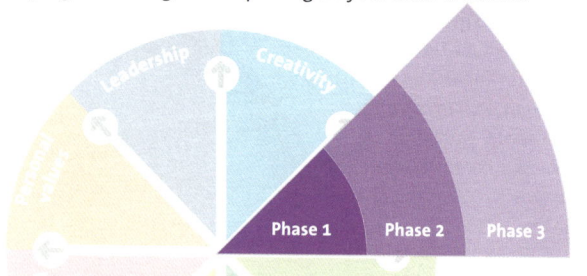

For every challenge you try, you will find lots of support. You can work on your own, in a team or do both simultaneously – a group activity like decorating your meeting place could include different challenges for different people.

> Remember, you don't need to work in Phases or Octants, you can dip in and out of challenges as you please.

LOOK **WIDER** FOR **MORE** INFO **ON** PAGES **9–13** OF **THE** MAIN **FILE**.

My guiding values

Guiding offers you values by which you can live your life. One part of this is the Promise. It's up to you when you make your Promise and how you celebrate this special occasion. You don't have to make it to start Look Wider, but as you work through challenges, think about how what you've achieved is part of your Promise.

The Promise

I promise that I will do my best:
To love my God,
To serve the Queen and my country,
To help other people
and
To keep the Guide Law.

In making my Promise, I commit myself to:
- seeking spiritual development
- contributing to society
- living by a simple code, the Guide Law.

As a Senior Section member, I make a further commitment to be of service to my community.

LOOK **WIDER** FOR **MORE** INFO **ON** PAGES **7–8** OF **THE** MAIN **FILE**.

The Guide Law

1. A Guide is honest, reliable and can be trusted.
2. A Guide is helpful, and uses her time and abilities wisely.
3. A Guide faces challenge and learns from her experiences.
4. A Guide is a good friend and a sister to all Guides.
5. A Guide is polite and considerate.
6. A Guide respects all living things and takes care of the world around her.

Promise required

Some specific Senior Section challenges, awards and training opportunities require you to make or renew your Promise. These are:

- Chief Guide's Challenge
- Queen's Guide Award
- Module 2 of the Leadership Qualification.

Helping hands

> You'll find plenty of guidance, support and encouragement with all your Look Wider challenges.

Leader
Your Leader is your first port of call. The more you involve her, the more you'll get out of the relationship as you get to know one another and build up trust.

Senior Section Group
Whether you're working on your own, with someone else or in a group, your peers can be a tower of strength. Tap into the resources of your entire Senior Section Group.

Challenge support group
For every challenge you'll pull together others who can support you. These could be friends working on the challenge, plus Advisers and others with specialist knowledge. The choice is yours!

Contacts
For each challenge you tackle, you'll develop useful contacts. There's space in this organiser to note their details. These could be people from guiding or other organisations, peers or professionals. Some of them may be contacts for life.

LOOK **WIDER** FOR **MORE** INFO ON PAGES **52–53** OF **THE MAIN FILE**.

My long-term goals

Think about your future. What are your dreams and long-term goals?

My future dreams

Use the diagram on page 15 to note what you want to be or achieve. Add more lines if you need to – and as your dreams change, come back and update it. That way you can always put your finger on your aspirations and monitor your progress towards a particular goal.

- Run a camp
- Travel in South America and understand the cultures
- Find out about becoming a councillor
- Become a proficient cook

Things I'd like for me in the future.

Think of this chart as a compass by which you can find your way if you lose sight of your goals.

14 LOOK WIDER FOR MORE INFO ON PAGES 54–55 OF THE MAIN FILE.

Directions for my future

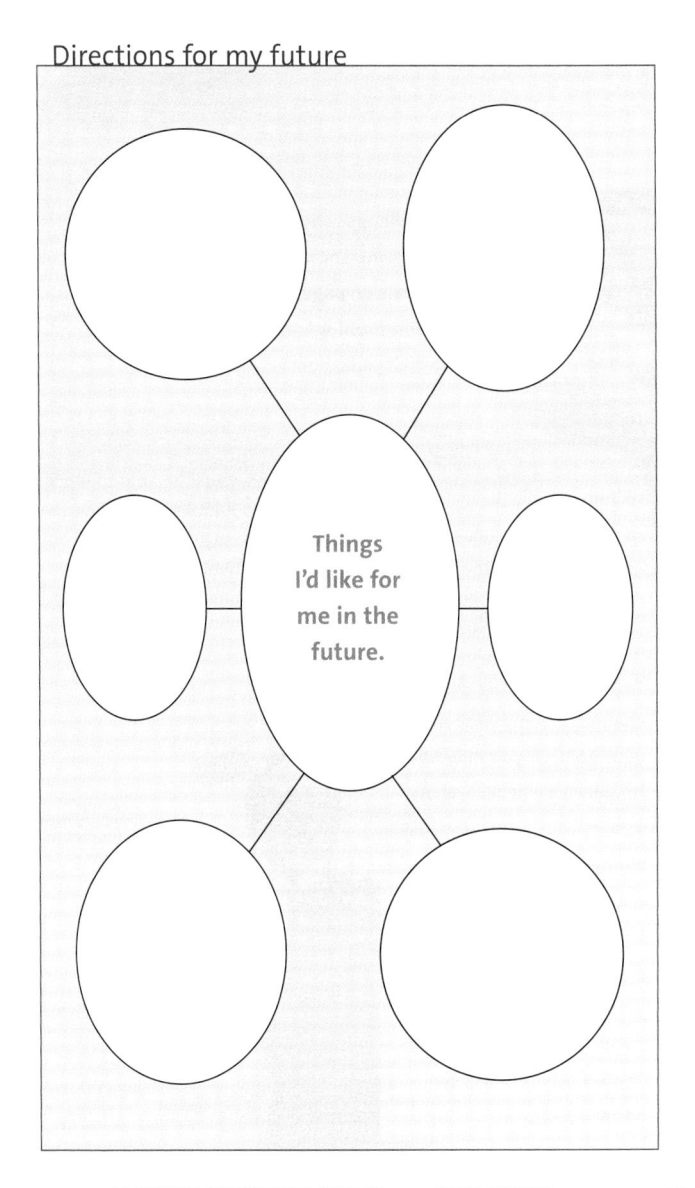

Things I'd like for me in the future.

LOOK **WIDER** FOR **MORE** INFO **ON** PAGES **54–55** OF **THE** MAIN **FILE**.

Choosing a challenge

Your challenges should link to your personal development. Look back at your dreams and aspirations on page 15 and think about the goals you could set yourself to reach them.

Matching challenges

By thinking through your dreams, you'll be able to work out the type of challenge you should take on. Decide which Octants are relevant and identify challenges from them that could help you. Alternatively, brainstorm challenge ideas with your Look Wider Team, or make up your own.

You could be lucky and one challenge helps you reach your goal. Or you may have to have a go at several. As you try challenges you may change your dreams. Take a look at pages 25–26 for how to tackle your planning. Always evaluate your challenges and make a record of what you did. There's more on this on pages 27–29.

LOOK **WIDER** FOR **MORE** INFO **ON** PAGES **56–61** OF **THE** MAIN FILE.

Ask myself

What do I want to do?

What does it mean to me?

Why do I want to do it?

Where am I now?

How far am I from achieving my goal(s)?

How can I do it?

What do I need to do to make it happen?

Who can help?

By what date do I want to do it?

Copy this page if you want to question each goal or dream.

LOOK **WIDER** FOR **MORE** INFO **ON** PAGES **56–61** OF **THE** MAIN FILE.

Personal plans

Use this diagram to plan how you'll make your Look Wider challenges work for you. It summarises the planning cycle which is at the heart of your Look Wider programme. Refer to it each time you take up a challenge. Keep coming back to it so you can take what you learn from one challenge and apply it to the next.

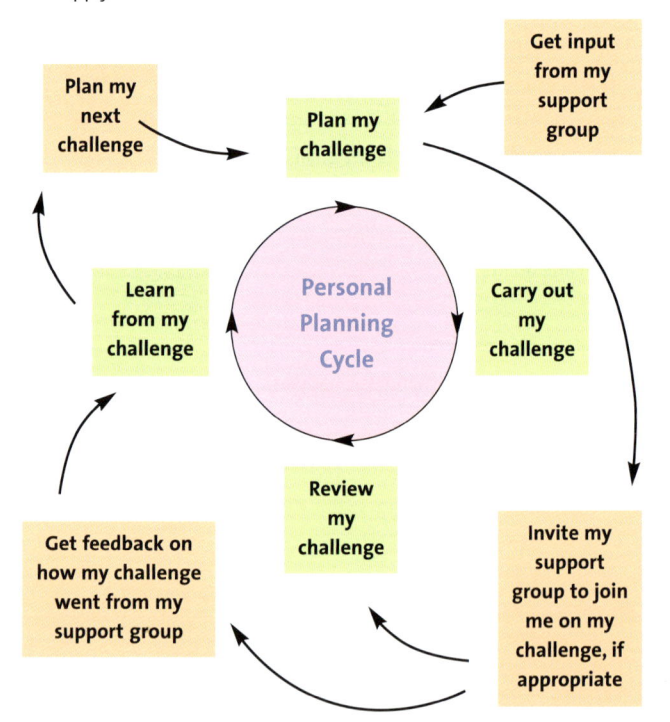

Personal Planning Cycle

- Plan my challenge
  - Get input from my support group
- Carry out my challenge
- Invite my support group to join me on my challenge, if appropriate
- Review my challenge
- Get feedback on how my challenge went from my support group
- Learn from my challenge
- Plan my next challenge

LOOK **WIDER** FOR **MORE** INFO **ON** PAGES **56–61** OF **THE** MAIN FILE.

Understanding
my strengths

Start to find out how you learn. Try to use what you learn to make the most of your Look Wider opportunity. Enjoy!

My learning style?

What are you like most of the time?	Yes	No
1 Give me directions, not a map!	○	○
2 Please show me before I have a go myself.	○	○
3 You'd better do a drawing to explain that.	○	○
4 My memory's better than my note taking.	○	○
5 I love taking things apart and putting them back together.	○	○
6 I'll have a go and learn from my mistakes.	○	○
7 Let me get a book on it!	○	○
8 It's amazing what you learn by listening to others.	○	○
9 I'm a hands-on type of person.	○	○

Find out what kind of learner you are on page 20.

LOOK WIDER FOR MORE INFO ON PAGES 66–70 OF THE MAIN FILE.

How do I learn?

We all favour one or two ways of making sense of information. Your answers on page 19 can indicate how you learn.

> An **auditory learner** answers 'Yes' to 1, 4 and 8: you learn by hearing, so may be good at languages.
>
> A **visual learner** answers 'Yes' to 2, 3 and 7: you learn by seeing, so respond to colour and images.
>
> A **kinesthetic learner** answers 'Yes' to 5, 6 and 9: you learn by doing, so objects and actions are important to how you learn.

Learning from it

By understanding which learning style or styles come naturally to you, you can see where your strengths lie. Think about the skills you want to master, and what's the best way for you to learn them. For instance don't try to learn from books, if a CD-Rom or hands-on approach is your preferred method.

> **Similarly you can take on challenges to develop your less-preferred learning style!**

LOOK **WIDER** FOR **MORE** INFO **ON** PAGES **66–70** OF **THE** MAIN FILE.

My communication style

For each pair of words below, score '1' for the word that best describes you. If you can't decide, score '1/2' against each word.

I tend to be...

challenging	accepting
to-the-point	indirect
fast-paced	slow-paced
demanding	thoughtful
active	relaxed
impatient	patient
bold	hesitant
decisive	studied
competitive	cooperative
confronting	receptive
Assertiveness totals ___	___
outgoing	guarded
approachable	distant
random	focused
unstructured	organised
intuitive	logical
open	controlled
casual	businesslike
warm	cool
friendly	formal
animated	unresponsive
Responsiveness totals ___	___

Use the totals to locate your position on the communication chart on page 22.

LOOK **WIDER** FOR **MORE** INFO **ON** PAGES **66–70** OF **THE** MAIN FILE.

21

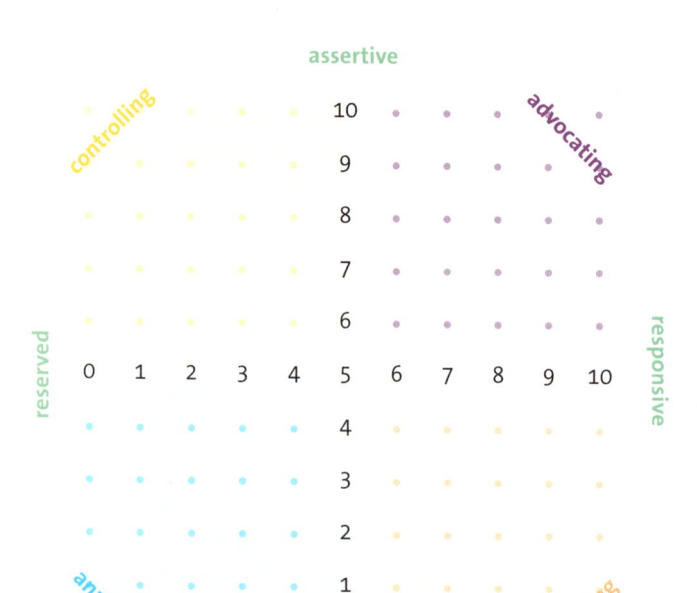

Communication chart

```
                          assertive

        controlling                              advocating
                            10
                             9
                             8
                             7
                             6
reserved  0  1  2  3  4      5   6  7  8  9  10    responsive
                             4
                             3
                             2
        analyzing            1                   facilitating
                             0

                          receptive
```

LOOK **WIDER** FOR **MORE** INFO **ON** PAGES **66–70** OF **THE MAIN FILE**.

What kind of communicator am I?

Controlling
○ **Attributes** Fast-paced, structured, practical, competitive, rational and focused.
○ **Negative appearances** Tough and demanding with little time for others.
○ **How to neutralise** Ease up and show more interest by listening more and showing appreciation!

Advocating
○ **Attributes** Fast-paced, unstructured, emotional, risk-tolerant, impatient and changeable.
○ **Negative appearances** Unreliable, light-hearted, too busy, thinks too big.
○ **Ways to neutralise** Be patient, focused and serious; listen carefully, stick to point.

Your responses on page 22 can provide a rough guide to what communication style comes naturally to you. Find out how your position on the chart translates into your communication style.

assertive

controlling — advocating
reserved — responsive
analyzing — facilitating

receptive

LOOK **WIDER** FOR **MORE** INFO **ON** PAGES **66–70** OF **THE MAIN FILE**.

23

Analyzing
- **Attributes** Slow-paced, structured, logical, cautious and thorough.
- **Negative appearances** Someone with a hidden agenda who withholds information and resists openness.
- **Ways to neutralise** Say what you think and stop taking life so seriously!

Facilitating
- **Attributes** Slow-paced, unstructured, people-oriented, cooperative, likes conversation and harmony.
- **Negative appearances** Unwilling to break bad news, someone who's not at ease with criticism.
- **Ways to neutralise** Stick up for your views and try to stop sugar-coating life!

Use the results to develop your communication style in a positive way! For example, if you're a 'controlling' person, networking probably won't come easily, so accept a challenge that'll make you more open to people.

Like the learning style quiz on page 19, come back to this chart in the future to see if you have changed.

LOOK **WIDER** FOR **MORE** INFO **ON** PAGES **66–70** OF **THE MAIN FILE**.

Active planning

With a good plan, you can divide a great leap into easy manageable steps. For every challenge, draw up an action plan like this one making small action steps (or targets) you need to achieve. Think carefully about their order and give each a realistic date.

Matching challenge

My dream To publish recipes
Challenge Soup it up! (Page 16 main file.)

For every step that takes you closer to your dreams, you may need to take on a challenge. Or one challenge may cover several steps.

Step 6
Structure material. Follow up letters.
Date 10-15 Feb

Step 5
Compile info on computer. Send out promo recipe with letter.
Date 28 Jan – 10 Feb

Step 4
Cost recipes and check variety. Fine tune. Second tasting.
Date 26-27 Jan

Step 3
Work out recipes. Tasting session. Get to grips with computer. Target mags/papers/publishers.
Date 12-25 Jan

Step 2
Search publisher's names. Ask Public Relations Adviser for support.
Date 7-12 Jan

Step 1
Brainstorm taste ideas.
Date 4-6 Jan

LOOK **WIDER** FOR **MORE** INFO **ON** PAGES **56-61** OF **THE MAIN FILE**.

Simple steps

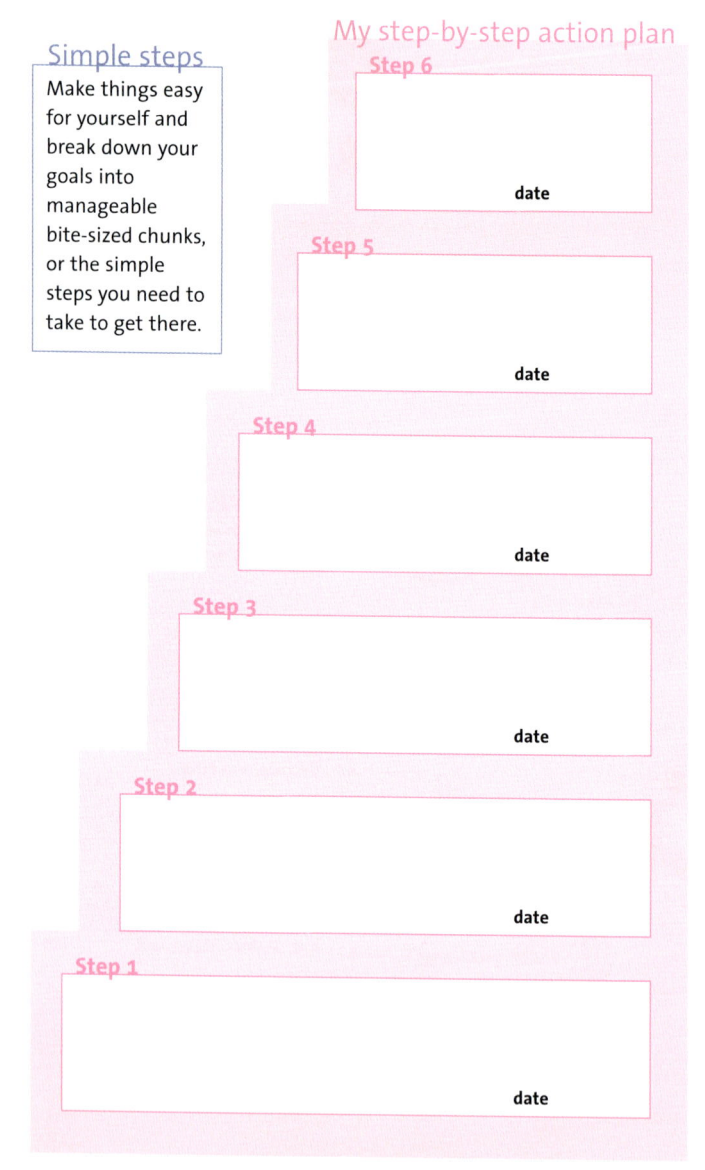

Make things easy for yourself and break down your goals into manageable bite-sized chunks, or the simple steps you need to take to get there.

My step-by-step action plan

Step 6

date

Step 5

date

Step 4

date

Step 3

date

Step 2

date

Step 1

date

LOOK **WIDER** FOR **MORE** INFO **ON** PAGES **56–61** OF **THE** MAIN **FILE**.

Am I making progress?

Continual evaluation of your goals and action plans form an essential part of Look Wider. Each time you complete (and start) a challenge, refer back to the planning cycle on page 18. Remember every challenge is individual – and so is every person. Your peers, your Look Wider Team and your challenge support group can provide crucial feedback. Remember that your success depends on what you wanted to get out of it.

Ask yourself
- Have I achieved all I wanted to?
- What went better than expected?
- What, if anything, didn't go to plan? What went wrong?
- What have I learned? Can I do anything I couldn't do before?
- Who has it brought me into contact with?
- What have I learned about myself?
- Would I do anything different? If so, what?
- What tips would I give to someone doing a similar challenge?
- What points will I take on board for my next challenge?

Look back to look wider
Every so often revisit your dreams and aspirations on page 15, as well as the communication and learning styles quizzes. Have you changed? Update these pages so you can see how you have moved forward by looking wider.

LOOK **WIDER** FOR **MORE** INFO **ON** PAGES **56–61** OF THE MAIN **FILE**.

Answering my challenges

Copy this page and fill it in to keep you on track. Don't forget to make a note of your challenge achievements for each Octant Phase on pages 30–61.

Have I achieved all I wanted to?

What went better than expected?

What, if anything, didn't go to plan? What went wrong?

What have I learned? Can I do anything I couldn't do before?

Who has it brought me into contact with?

What have I learned about myself?

Would I do anything different? If so, what?

What tips would I give to someone doing a similar challenge?

What points will I take on board for my next challenge?

Getting going

On pages 30–61 you'll find more information about each Octant, plus space to record your thrills and spills. At the start of each Octant, you'll find sample challenges to give you an idea of the ground it covers.

Recording my development

Record anything that's relevant to your challenge. There are four pages for every Octant, with space for all three Phases. For a quick review of every challenge, simply tick the appropriate symbol giving it a thumbs-up, thumbs-down or not-so-sure. Then make any notes you want, or even stick in photos.

Building up contacts

There's space to list peers, professionals and organisations who have helped you. Build up a network of contacts – don't just collect names! Try to develop mutually-beneficial relationships and be active in helping others develop contacts, too.

Keep a note of the Phases you do for each Octant on this tick chart.

	Phase 1	Phase 2	Phase 3
Creativity	◯	◯	◯
Fit for life	◯	◯	◯
Community action	◯	◯	◯
Out of doors	◯	◯	◯
International	◯	◯	◯
Independent living	◯	◯	◯
Personal values	◯	◯	◯
Leadership	◯	◯	◯

LOOK WIDER FOR MORE INFO ON PAGES 56–61 OF THE MAIN FILE.

Create your dreams

This Octant is your chance to exercise your imagination and make the most of your creativeness. Feel free to express yourself.

Creative challenge ideas

Cook up a feast for family or friends. Plan a special three-course meal with wine, or invent your own designer drink! Find out which wine(s) you should serve. Why not go the whole hog and make it a black-tie affair?

Tell the world about your unit or about guiding in general. Create your own web pages and launch a site into cyberspace.

Seek new heights! Improve your circus skills and your confidence with a circus skills workshop.

Explore your hidden potential: check out the latest colour-analysis techniques. Find out which colours really suit you and design a whole new wardrobe for yourself – use pictures from old magazines if your sketching isn't up to scratch.

Get to grips with a camcorder. Learn how to operate one and use it to capture your next Look Wider challenge on film.

Find out about the ancient art of Feng Shui and free up the flow of energy in your home!

TAKE UP THE CHALLENGE FROM STACKS OF IDEAS IN THE MAIN IDEA PAGES 16–19).

Phase 1

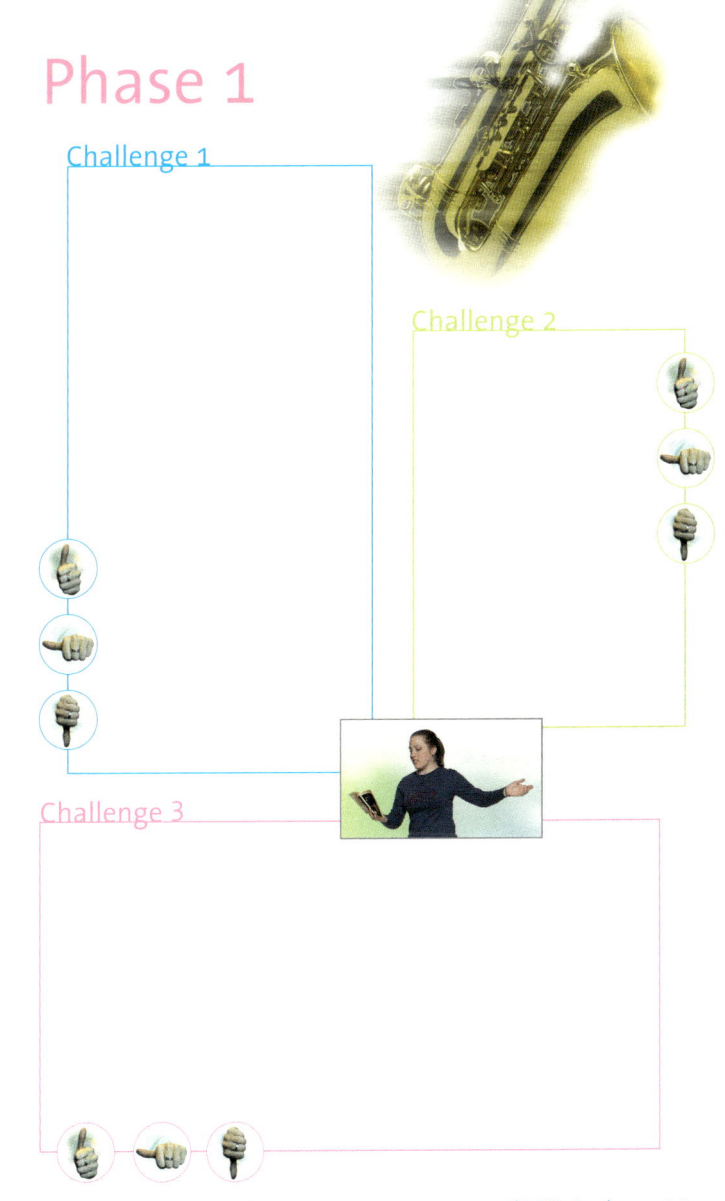

Challenge 1

Challenge 2

Challenge 3

TAKE UP THE CHALLENGE FROM STACKS OF IDEAS IN THE MAIN FILE (PAGES 16–19).

Phase 2

Phase 3

TAKE UP **THE** CHALLENGE **FROM** STACKS **OF** IDEAS **IN THE MAIN** FILE (**PAGES** 16–19).

Creative contacts

| Name |
| Address |
| Postcode |
| ☎ Mobile |
| Email |

| Name |
| Address |
| Postcode |
| ☎ Mobile |
| Email |

| Name |
| Address |
| Postcode |
| ☎ Mobile |
| Email |

| Name |
| Address |
| Postcode |
| ☎ Mobile |
| Email |

Health and happiness

This Octant looks at the building blocks of healthy living. It encourages you to take an interest in what you eat and how you choose to live your life.

Fit for life challenge ideas

Make a decision to take the stairs from now on, never the lift. Challenge friends to do the same and see how long you can last without using a lift.

Throw a party to put friends in the pink! Serve colourful non-alcoholic drinks and delicious healthy snacks. Prepare copies of your recipes to hand out to your friends.

Check out your local Well Woman Clinic and find out what they can offer you.

Stretch yourself! Try a new form of exercise, e.g. aerobics, callanetics, pilates, stretch, yoga, T'ai Chi.

Jump-start your day! Find out about your chakras (bodily centres of spiritual power)... and try to boost them!

Have fun and get fit at the same time. Go swimming or line-dancing with a friend.

TAKE UP THE CHALLENGE FROM STACKS OF IDEAS IN THE MAIN FILE (PAGES 20–23).

Phase 1

Challenge 1

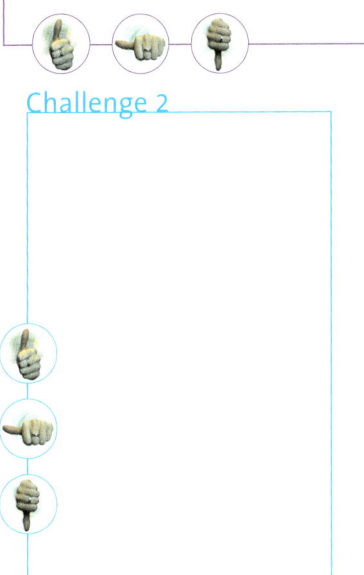

Challenge 2

Challenge 3

TAKE UP **THE** CHALLENGE **FROM** STACKS **OF** IDEAS **IN** THE **MAIN** FILE (**PAGES** 20–23).

Phase 2

Phase 3

36 TAKE UP THE CHALLENGE FROM STACKS OF IDEAS IN THE MAIN FILE (PAGES 20–23).

Fit for life contacts

| Name |
| Address |
| Postcode |
| ☎ Mobile |
| Email |

| Name |
| Address |
| Postcode |
| ☎ Mobile |
| Email |

| Name |
| Address |
| Postcode |
| ☎ Mobile |
| Email |

| Name |
| Address |
| Postcode |
| ☎ Mobile |
| Email |

HANG ON TO **THIS** PAGE **FOR** USE **IN** YOUR **FUTURE**.

Action for others

This Octant encourages you to identify local concerns and to get things done. It helps you to establish partnerships and encourage decision-making.

Community action challenge ideas

How far can you get from your front door on £10 (or equivalent)? Don't forget you need to get home again – hitchhiking is not allowed!

Find out if there's a Young Carer Group in your area and what you can do to help.

Sleep under the stars for a night to raise funds and awareness for a charity that helps homeless young people, e.g. Crisis.

Find out about 'talking newspapers' and help to produce a copy on issues concerning young people.

Learn a skill you can share with others in your community, e.g. first aid, childcare, community sports, event management, babysitting.

Identify community needs. Talk to people about the importance of not making assumptions about what is needed or not being catered for.

38   TAKE UP THE CHALLENGE FROM STACKS OF IDEAS IN THE MAIN FILE (PAGES 24–27).

Phase 1

Challenge 1

Challenge 2

Challenge 3

TAKE UP THE CHALLENGE FROM STACKS OF IDEAS IN THE MAIN FILE (PAGES 24–27).

Phase 2

Phase 3

TAKE UP **THE** CHALLENGE **FROM** STACKS **OF** IDEAS **IN** THE **MAIN** FILE (**PAGES** 24–27).

Community action contacts

Name

Address

Postcode

☎	Mobile

Email

Name

Address

Postcode

☎	Mobile

Email

Name

Address

Postcode

☎	Mobile

Email

Name

Address

Postcode

☎	Mobile

Email

HANG ONTO **THIS** PAGE FOR USE **IN** YOUR FUTURE.

Get out and have fun

The Outdoors covers abseiling to zoology. Find out more about the natural world we live in, identify environmental issues and play your part in saving our planet.

Outdoor challenge ideas

Embrace the art of bouldering, then do some weaselling... find out what you can and have a go!

Under wraps: try growing something from seed for the first time.

Work outdoors abroad. Do grape picking in France, go on a dig in northern Spain, work on a cattle ranch in Australia, become a Swiss chalet girl, be a holiday rep in Greece or work at a US summer camp!

Get involved in an outdoor community project (e.g. restoring a garden) or do some voluntary work outdoors: be a conservation volunteer, park ranger, summer playworker or support worker for a disabled person on an outdoor break.

Be on the lookout for a local outdoor activity club. Visit one, with a view to joining. Consider abseiling, boating, caving, conservation, drystone walling, gardening, rowing, running, sailing or windsurfing.

Organise the planting of trees on an exposed hillside to prevent soil erosion.

TAKE UP THE CHALLENGE FROM STACKS OF IDEAS IN THE MAIN FILE (PAGES 28–31).

Phase 1

Challenge 1

Challenge 2

Challenge 3

TAKE UP THE CHALLENGE FROM STACKS OF IDEAS IN THE MAIN FILE (PAGES 28–31).

Phase 2

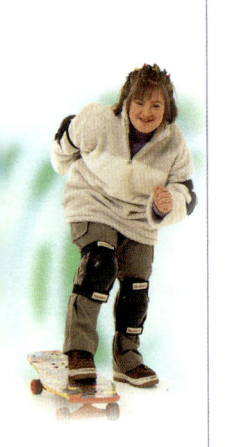

Phase 3

TAKE UP THE CHALLENGE FROM STACKS OF IDEAS IN THE MAIN FILE (PAGES 28–31).

Out of doors contacts

Name

Address

Postcode

☎ Mobile

Email

Name

Address

Postcode

☎ Mobile

Email

Name

Address

Postcode

☎ Mobile

Email

Name

Address

Postcode

☎ Mobile

Email

HANG ONTO **THIS** PAGE **FOR** USE **IN** YOUR **FUTURE**.

World vision

International lets you explore the world and build an understanding and awareness of peoples, cultures and beliefs. Find out about the global issues and where you stand.

International challenge ideas

Find out what your local twin town (city or village) scheme has to offer. Arrange an exchange with Guides there or join a community-based exchange programme.

Fair's fair! Contact a supermarket and ask about their Fair Trade policies. Research how much a cocoa worker gets for a week's work and compare that to how much a bar of chocolate costs you.

Examine how the lives of leading figures such as Nelson Mandela, Mother Teresa, Mahatma Gandhi and Dr Martin Luther King have changed our world. What messages did they pass on? Write a paper or give a lecture on how people can change the world, or discuss what you've learned with family and friends.

Plan a journey around a theme or something quirky, e.g. take a short holiday on a tall ship, follow in someone's footsteps, visit European capitals, or birthplaces of people you admire.

Attend or take part in a cultural festival – at home or abroad.

Hold a discussion on rights. What is meant by 'basic human rights'? How are they interpreted in different countries?

Phase 1

Challenge 1

Challenge 2

Challenge 3

TAKE UP THE CHALLENGE FROM STACKS OF IDEAS IN THE MAIN FILE (PAGES 32–35).

Phase 2

Phase 3

TAKE UP THE CHALLENGE FROM STACKS OF IDEAS IN THE MAIN FILE (PAGES 32–35).

International contacts

| Name |
| Address |
| Postcode |
| ☏ Mobile |
| Email |

| Name |
| Address |
| Postcode |
| ☏ Mobile |
| Email |

| Name |
| Address |
| Postcode |
| ☏ Mobile |
| Email |

| Name |
| Address |
| Postcode |
| ☏ Mobile |
| Email |

HANG ONTO **THIS** PAGE **FOR** USE **IN** YOUR **FUTURE.**

Right moves for me

This Octant encourages you to look at, prepare for and meet the challenges of an independent life.

Independent living challenge ideas

Get some tips on making a good impression: ask the personnel manager of a local company to come along and talk to your group about interview techniques.

Find out what difference your vote can make. How can you encourage young people in your area to vote?

Do a basic car-maintenance course or ask a local mechanic to give your group a lesson. Find out how to use a dipstick, change your oil, check your tyres, recharge a battery, clean your plugs and change a wheel.

Compare brand-name goods with non-brand goods. Look at prices and what you get for them. When does price matter less or more than quality? Do non-brand goods pass the blindfold taste test?

Consider the pros and cons of becoming a parent at the ages of 16, 18, 30 and 45.

Think about how you respond to stressful situations. Identify one reaction you'd like to change, e.g. anger, palpitations, breathlessness, sweating, stammering and work to overcome it.

Phase 1

Challenge 2

Challenge 1

Challenge 3

TAKE UP THE CHALLENGE FROM STACKS OF IDEAS IN THE MAIN FILE (PAGES 36-39)

Phase 2

Phase 3

TAKE UP **THE** CHALLENGE **FROM** STACKS **OF** IDEAS **IN THE MAIN** FILE **(PAGES** 36–39).

Independent living contacts

| Name |
| Address |
| Postcode |
| ☎ | Mobile |
| Email |

| Name |
| Address |
| Postcode |
| ☎ | Mobile |
| Email |

| Name |
| Address |
| Postcode |
| ☎ | Mobile |
| Email |

| Name |
| Address |
| Postcode |
| ☎ | Mobile |
| Email |

You are who you are

Personal values encourages you to think about life's options. Sort out and seek out the things that matter to you in life and work out who you are.

Personal values challenge ideas

Make a list of skills you have and skills you want. Discuss your lists with someone who knows you well. Prioritise the skills you'd like to have and decide how you're going to develop them.

Put together a collection of quotes, quips and extracts that you find inspirational, then do something creative with them – publish them in a book or on the web, or hold a reading event.

List 12 qualities you'd look for in a partner. Arrange them according to their importance. Ask friends to do the same and compare lists.

What do you get out of guiding? Think about the positive images of guiding. Are there things you would change? Is there room for improvement and if so, where?

Spend part of a day in silence reflecting on your beliefs. Allow time for reading, being creative, walking and thinking. In the evening meet up for a meal with a group of friends and discuss your experiences.

Not feeling quite yourself? Think about ways you might conform to stereotypes. Consider whether you've chosen this or been pressurised into it. Is there anything about yourself that you'd like to change?

TAKE UP THE CHALLENGE FROM STACKS OF IDEAS IN THE MAIN FILE (PAGES 40–43).

Phase 1

Challenge 1

Challenge 2

Challenge 3

TAKE UP THE CHALLENGE FROM STACKS OF IDEAS IN THE MAIN FILE (PAGES 40–43)

Phase 2

Phase 3

TAKE UP **THE** CHALLENGE **FROM** STACKS **OF** IDEAS **IN** THE **MAIN** FILE (**PAGES** 40–43).

56

Personal values contacts

| Name |
| Address |
| Postcode |
| ☎ Mobile |
| Email |

| Name |
| Address |
| Postcode |
| ☎ Mobile |
| Email |

| Name |
| Address |
| Postcode |
| ☎ Mobile |
| Email |

| Name |
| Address |
| Postcode |
| ☎ Mobile |
| Email |

HANG ONTO **THIS** PAGE **FOR** USE **IN** YOUR **FUTURE**.

Lead the way

You can use this Octant to explore your leadership potential in any role you choose. It helps you to develop opportunities and to identify the skills and qualities a good leader needs.

Leadership challenge ideas

Think of a leadership skill you'd like to develop, e.g. to be more inspirational, more able to take the flak – and take steps to work towards it.

Imagine recruiting your own football, hockey or softball team. Who would you choose and why?

People can be their own worst enemy where self-esteem is concerned. Work with a group of Brownies or Guides on a project designed to help them build theirs.

Words aren't everything. Investigate non-verbal communication so you can use it and learn to interpret other people's reactions.

Organise an event to pass on something you've learned, e.g. a sport, art form, language, software programme, information or resources.

Always late? Turn over a new leaf – discover the joys of time management and get there on time!

Phase 1

Challenge 1

Challenge 2

Challenge 3

TAKE UP THE CHALLENGE FROM STACKS OF IDEAS IN THE MAIN FILE (PAGES 44–49)

Phase 2

Phase 3

60 TAKE UP THE CHALLENGE FROM STACKS OF IDEAS IN THE MAIN FILE (PAGES 44–49).

Leadership contacts

Name
Address
Postcode
☎ Mobile
Email

Name
Address
Postcode
☎ Mobile
Email

Name
Address
Postcode
☎ Mobile
Email

Name
Address
Postcode
☎ Mobile
Email

HANG ONTO **THIS** PAGE **FOR** USE **IN** YOUR **FUTURE**.

Take your chance

Life moves on, and so should you! You'll know by now that Look Wider offers hundreds of challenges, ideas and inspirations. But there's even more on offer to you as a Senior Section member, so take your chance to have a go at some.

Ways to keep looking wider

Look Wider is open to any young woman aged 14 to 25, but in what capacity is up to you. Take a look at these opportunities and remember just because you started Look Wider as, say, a Young Leader it doesn't mean to say you can't still follow it as a young Commissioner.

On pages 64–75 there is a fuller explanation of these opportunities and how you can grasp them. Don't be shy. Get out there and give it a go if you see something that you fancy!

A person to be
- Peer educator
- Ranger Guide
- Young Leader
- Adviser
- Commissioner
- Leader
- Trainer

MORE INFO ON PAGES 64–65 OF THE MAIN FILE. TAKE A LOOK WIDER.

Group dynamics
- British Youth Council delegate
- LINK member
- Student Scout and Guide Organisation (SSAGO) member
- Member of the Trefoil Guild
- Part of the Youth Forum
- House assistant

Fun overseas
- Represent Girlguiding UK internationally
- Participate in a GOLD project

More strings to your bow
Qualifications, courses, training and experience all give you an edge on others during life, so here are just some of the opportunities open to you.

- The Chief Guide's Challenge
- Queen's Guide Award
- The Duke of Edinburgh's Award
- Senior Section permits
- Making It Count
- The Commonwealth Award
- Girlguiding UK training opportunities, such as the leadership or training qualification, or camp, holiday, catering, climbing, health and first aid, walking, music and 1st Response emergency aid training schemes

Local opportunities
Find out from your Commissioner or Leader if there are any local opportunities, like being part of the organisation team for a large event. There may be other jobs on offer which you could try as well. Go ahead and ask!

MORE INFO **ON** PAGES **64-65** OF **THE MAIN FILE.** TAKE **A** LOOK **WIDER.**

Take on a new role

Do you fancy a change? Do you want to take your skills into a new role? There's a range of things on offer to you, so talk to your Leader and Commissioner about openings locally.

Peer educator

A peer educator informs others using activities about the issues and concerns they may have, e.g. bullying, substance abuse or women's health. It's a good introduction to training plus a chance to gain organisational and people skills.

My local peer education contact

| Name |
| Address |
| Postcode |
| ( ) Mobile |
| Email |

Alternatively, contact the Senior Section Team at CHQ (see page 6) or email seniorsection@girlguiding.org.uk.

Ranger Guide

Rangers meet together in a unit run by a Look Wider Team – with help from the rest of the unit and their Leader. If there isn't a unit nearby, you can still take part as a lone Ranger keeping in touch with your Leader by email, phone or snail mail.

64 SKILLS FOR LIFE. TAKE YOUR CHANCE. ALWAYS LOOK WIDER.

My local Ranger Guide contact

Name

Address

Postcode

☎ Mobile

Email

Young Leader

Young Leaders can work with Rainbows, Brownies or Guides as part of the leader team. They follow Making It Count, or the Association's Leadership Qualification (as well as Look Wider) learning about running a unit and developing leadership skills.

My local Young Leader contact

Name

Address

Postcode

☎ Mobile

Email

If you're 16 or over, make sure you've filled in your W/R form and got your Safe From Harm card.

Adviser

From your 18th birthday you can be an Adviser. Each Division and County has Advisers, who work in a team with Leaders and the Commissioner. They cover all aspects of guiding in that area and are appointed for five years. If you're a practical person who gets things done, as well as being a good team-player with great people skills, this role can take you a step further

SKILLS FOR **LIFE**. TAKE **YOUR** CHANCE. **ALWAYS** LOOK **WIDER**.

Commissioner

The Commissioner supports guiding locally. She takes an overview of everything from training requirements to safety, managing finances to recruitment and retention. She does this by establishing a team to support her. It's a full-on management role, which you need to be 18 to do. You'll receive training and support so it's a great opportunity if management is what you want to get into.

Leader

Again, a role for when you reach 18. It's guiding at the sharp end – but where ALL the fun is! It's up to you to deliver the programme, but you get all the feedback, the laughs, the thrills and spills that come with working with girls and young women. There is a Leadership Qualification and lots of support to help you, plus a range of other training opportunities.

Trainer

Another one for over 18s that is a good step if you're interested in training and development. The Association offers a competence-based assessment course. You'll have a tutor to help you as well as your local Training Support Group. The qualification is recognised nationally outside guiding, but relies on the ethos of guiding. You could even qualify for an OCR training award. Either way, a big plus on your CV!

Make contact

For more details about becoming an Adviser, Commissioner, Leader or trainer, contact your Commissioner (see page 4).

Group dynamics

British Youth Council delegate

The BYC is the voice of young people and represents 16–25 year olds, taking their views to government, decision-makers and the media. It consists of youth organisations, clubs and unions, and Girlguiding UK has a delegation of 18 members. It's a chance to have your voice heard and make a difference.

Contact

Marketing and Communications at CHQ (see page 6) or www.byc.org.uk.

LINK member

LINK International Fellowship offers social events, outdoor activities, training opportunities and the chance to get involved in service projects. It has a flexible framework for you to keep in touch with guiding.

National contact

LINK at CHQ (see page 6) ☎ 020 7592 1844 (24-hour answerphone) E-mail linkuk@link-uk.org or info@link-uk.org

My local LINK contact

Name
Address
Postcode
☎ Mobile
Email

SKILLS FOR LIFE. TAKE YOUR CHANCE. ALWAYS LOOK WIDER.

Student Scout and Guide Organisation

SSAGO provides an exciting way of keeping in touch with guiding at college or university. Many colleges and universities have a club, but you can join as an individual member. SSAGO offers a huge range of social events, outdoor activities and service opportunities.

National contact
SSAGO at CHQ (see page 6)
Email members@ssago.org.uk
Website www.ssago.org.uk.

My local SSAGO contact

| Name |
| Address |
| Postcode |
| Mobile |
| Email |

The Trefoil Guild

The Trefoil Guild offers a great chance to meet people with a genuine enthusiasm for guiding and a wealth of skills and experience they are willing to share. Guilds usually support the work of the District as well as offering a range of social events and outdoor opportunities to get stuck into as well.

National contact

The Trefoil Guild at CHQ (see page 6) 020 7592 1844 (24-hour answerphone) Email trefoilguild@girlguiding.org.uk

My local Trefoil Guild contact

Name

Address

Postcode

Mobile

Email

Youth Forum

If you want to work on Association projects, debate real issues plus develop new skills for yourself then the Youth Forum is for you. This annual event is aimed at young women and organised by a Senior Section planning team. Details are published in *Guiding magazine* and on Girlguiding UK's website.

National contact

Youth Forum at CHQ (see page 6)
Email seniorsection@girlguiding.org.uk

My local Youth Forum contact

Name

Address

Postcode

Mobile

Email

House assistant

You can join the team at one of Girlguiding UK's Training and Activity Centres, or at a World Centre, as a house assistant. The role offers an excellent way to get hands-on experience in the leisure industry and is a fun way to spend a gap year.

More information

Contact the appropriate centre direct. Addresses can be found at www.girlguiding.org.uk or in *The Guiding Manual*.

SKILLS FOR LIFE. TAKE YOUR CHANCE. ALWAYS LOOK WIDER.

Fun overseas

Be representative
Girlguiding UK regularly sends representatives to WAGGGS' seminars, Europe Region meetings and international conferences. You need to be aged 18 or over and go through a selection procedure. You are expected to attend certain events, and to report back on the discussions or workshops you took part in so knowledge and experience can be shared with others.

Contact
Guiding Development at CHQ (see page 6)
Email international@girlguiding.org.uk.

GOLD
GOLD, or Guiding Overseas Linked with Development, is a chance for you to make a difference while working alongside Guides in another country. You need to be 18 or over to take part in GOLD.

As well as encouraging the development of guiding and cultural exchanges, it offers a great challenge to all participants plus an opportunity to exchange skills and knowledge.

Selection
You start at a GOLD INTOPS selection weekend where you'll encounter challenges and fun. GOLD INTOPS usually take place round the country in the autumn. To find out more:
○ get in touch with your International Adviser
○ contact international@girlguiding.org.uk or call 020 7834 6242
○ keep an eye on the news in *Guiding magazine*.

More
strings to your bow

The Chief Guide's Challenge
If you complete Phases 1 and 2 of every Octant and make or renew your Promise, you'll receive the Chief Guide's Challenge certificate. It's an opportunity to look back over your achievements so far and look forward to the future.

Check your progress through the Phases on page 27.

Queen's Guide Award
This award is an opportunity to play an active role in both local and wider communities, as well as guiding. There is continual assessment by your peers and Guider with a presentation at the end. You do need to make or renew your Promise. Successful candidates are invited to a national presentation of the award.

Activities chosen for Look Wider can also go towards your Queen's Guide Award.

County Queen's Guide Coordinator
Name

Address

Postcode

☏ Mobile

Email

SKILLS FOR LIFE. TAKE YOUR CHANCE. ALWAYS LOOK WIDER.

Duke of Edinburgh's Award

You can take part in the Duke of Edinburgh's Award. There are three Awards to work towards:
- Bronze (for over 14 year-olds).
- Silver (for over 15 year-olds).
- Gold (for over 16 year-olds).

Each Award covers four areas – service, expedition, skills and physical recreation. For the Gold Award there is also a residential project. You must start working on an Award before your 23rd birthday.

County Duke of Edinburgh's Award Adviser

| Name |
| Address |
| Postcode |
| ☎ Mobile |
| Email |

Senior Section Permit

If you'd like to gain a qualification so you can run a camp or holiday for other Senior Section members, or Guides, you know take a look at pages 76–96 for all the information.

Making It Count

Making It Count is Girlguiding UK's leadership scheme for 14 and 15 year olds and it's not just for Young Leaders. It's hand-on and aims to give you knowledge, skills and experience which you can build on if you decide to work through Girlguiding UK's Leadership Qualification (see page 74).

Commonwealth Award

The Commonwealth Award is open to older Guides and Senior Section members in all Commonwealth countries. A copy of the syllabus can be found on pages 107–108 of the main *Look Wider* file.

SKILLS FOR LIFE. TAKE YOUR CHANCE. ALWAYS LOOK WIDER.

Training opportunities

Girlguiding UK qualifications and schemes are competence-based, so all training and assessment relies on you learning skills and knowledge that you can demonstrate. To gain a qualification you need to work through a course, with the support of your Commissioner, plus local Guiders and trainers. Girlguiding UK publishes a series of booklets each containing a syllabus with space to record assessment.

Camp and holiday scheme

This is a must to take Brownies, Guides or Senior Section members on camp or holiday. There are seven licences to choose from, depending on the type of event and the section you work with. You need to be aged 18 or over and hold a Warrant or Appointment Card. (See also Senior Section Permit on page 72.)

County Camp Adviser

| Name |
| Address |
| Postcode |
| ☎ Mobile |
| Email |

County Holiday Adviser

| Name |
| Address |
| Postcode |
| ☎ Mobile |
| Email |

SKILLS FOR **LIFE.** TAKE **YOUR** CHANCE. **ALWAYS** LOOK **WIDER.**

Catering scheme

Again, this is for over 18s. Primarily it is for catering at camps and holidays and covers a wide range of issues from kitchen hygiene to menu preparation. A great start for anyone interested in a career in catering.

Health and first aid scheme

If you want to learn about maintaining good hygiene standards, as well as providing first aid at a residential event, then this is the thing for you. It'll be of real interest if you see your future in caring or health and safety roles. You need to be 18 or over.

County Outdoor Activities Adviser

| Name |
| Address |
| Postcode |
| ( ) Mobile |
| Email |

SKILLS FOR **LIFE**. TAKE **YOUR** CHANCE. **ALWAYS** LOOK **WIDER**.

Leadership qualification
Aimed at Young Leaders and new Leaders it'll enable you to be an effective member of the unit's leader team within six months or two terms. You need to be aged 16 or over and have completed form W/R. See pages 65 and 66 or speak to your Guider or Commissioner.

Training qualification
If you fancy being a trainer (see page 66), then this opportunity takes you there. You need to be at least 18 and have held a Warrant or Appointment Card for one year or more.

Walking scheme
This scheme is for members aged 14 plus and offers training on skills related to walking in a variety of terrains.

County Walking Adviser

| Name |
| Address |
| Postcode |
| ☎ Mobile |
| Email |

Other qualifications
There are a range of other qualifications and training opportunities on offer, such as canoeing, rowing, sailing, boardsailing, power cruising, climbing, music and 1st Response emergency aid training. Many offer you a head start if you are entering a relevant job or career in the outdoor education or leisure industries. For more information keep an eye on *Guiding magazine* and www.girlguiding.org.uk.

SKILLS FOR LIFE. TAKE YOUR CHANCE. ALWAYS LOOK WIDER.

Camps,
holidays and overnight events

> There are two types of Senior Section Permit that'll provide you with the skills and ability to take a small group away.

Overnight Permit
The Overnight Permit, as the name suggests, allows you to take up to eight Guides or Senior Section members on a camp or holiday that lasts up to 24 hours. It could start right after a weekly meeting and finish at breakfast the next day.

Senior Section Permit
This allows you to take up to eight Guides or Senior Section members away for two nights or more.

The others with you
With either permit you've got to know the others you're taking away. They should be Senior Section members or Guides you work closely with or know well. Anyone under 18 years of age needs parental consent. This can be obtained using form G/C, which is available from Girlguiding UK Trading Service. Don't forget a form for yourself as well, if you haven't reached 18.

Approval to do it
You must obtain the approval of your Senior Section Guider, Look Wider Team and relevant outdoor Advisers. The Adviser is usually the Camp Adviser but if, for example, you were planning a walking holiday or canal cruise, you'd have to talk to your Walking or Boating Adviser. If you are planning to take Guides away, you'll also need permission from their Guide Leader.

LOOK AT **YOURSELF** IN **THE** WIDER WORLD. DO **IT** WITH **LOOK** WIDER.

You can get all this done using form A/P which is available from Girlguiding UK Trading Service.

> Contact Girlguiding UK Trading Service at www.girlguiding.org.uk/shop or call 0161 941 2237.

Using your permit

Either permit may be used for:
- a base camp or holiday.
- a mobile expedition.

For an expedition you must hold, or be working to gain, the expedition module to your permit.

Other activities

If you want to have a go at activities like abseiling or boating, you'll need to make sure you have a suitably qualified or experienced instructor to lead the activity. This could be you, but if it isn't the person must be approved by your Leader or District Commissioner. So have her or his details ready when filling in form A/P. To find out what qualifications are needed, check the latest edition of *The Guiding Manual*.

Peer group residentials

There are ways in which you can go away without a permit. See the inside back cover for details of peer group residentials.

Getting your permit

Depending on the type of event you want to run, you need to complete certain modules from the following pages. Take a look at the table on page 79 to see which ones you need to do.

Every module consists of a set of requirements that you need to show an Assessor you can do or have done. You'll need to provide 'evidence' like booking confirmation letters or receipts for food. Evidence doesn't have to be formal, so don't worry about showing scribbled notes from a phone call. You will need to be organised when collecting evidence, as each piece must be numbered. You then need to make sure the right number is then written on the right recording page in the 'Ref no' space.

Assessment

Everyone is assessed against the same standard to make sure the process is fair. Your Assessor will hold an Association Camp or Holiday Licence. Your Assessor can't be your own Leader, though, or anyone else who you regularly do your guiding with.

Your Assessor

Ask your Leader to help you find an Assessor. Your Assessor's responsible for:

- checking her role, as outlined in *Training Opportunities: Camp and Holiday Scheme*.
- making arrangements to see you.
- negotiating opportunities for relevant experience/training for you.
- talking through any areas of concern either of you have.
- assessing and returning your evidence within agreed timescales.
- visiting your event.
- signing your assessment record.

You can be assessed at the same venue with another Senior Section member – even sharing activity sessions – provided that the events are planned and run separately.

Accrediting experience

If you held the Guide Camp Permit, or have suitable experience from outside guiding, you'll be accredited with this prior learning as felt appropriate by the Assessor. You should talk to her about this. Similarly, all the skills, knowledge and experience can be carried forward and accredited if you choose in the future to do any of the Association's camp or holiday licences (see page 73).

LOOK AT **YOURSELF** IN THE **WIDER WORLD.** DO **IT** WITH **LOOK** WIDER.

Modules required for each qualification

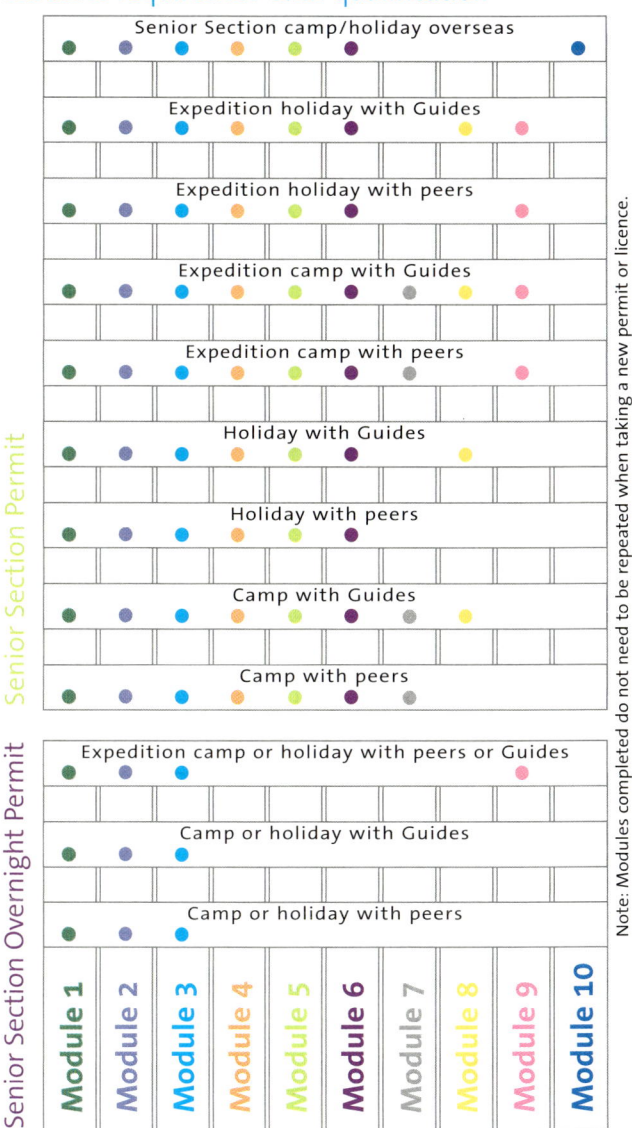

Qualification	M1	M2	M3	M4	M5	M6	M7	M8	M9	M10
Senior Section Permit										
Senior Section camp/holiday overseas	●	●	●	●	●	●				●
Expedition holiday with Guides	●	●	●	●	●	●		●	●	
Expedition holiday with peers	●	●	●	●	●	●			●	
Expedition camp with Guides	●	●	●	●	●	●	●	●		
Expedition camp with peers	●	●	●	●	●	●	●		●	
Holiday with Guides	●	●	●	●		●		●		
Holiday with peers	●	●	●		●	●				
Camp with Guides	●	●	●	●	●	●	●	●		
Camp with peers	●	●	●	●	●	●	●			
Senior Section Overnight Permit										
Expedition camp or holiday with peers or Guides	●	●	●						●	
Camp or holiday with Guides	●	●	●							
Camp or holiday with peers	●	●								

Note: Modules completed do not need to be repeated when taking a new permit or licence.

LOOK AT YOURSELF IN THE WIDER WORLD, DO IT WITH LOOK WIDER.

Module 1
plan a residential event

Element 1a: decide on the type of event
How do I achieve this?
i) Discuss the event with the Senior Section Leader, Guide Leader, Advisers and Commissioner, as appropriate.
ii) Discuss the event with participants and the Look Wider Team, where appropriate.
iii) Agree the purpose of, and objectives for, the event.
iv) Agree the type of event and the programme content.
v) Ensure chosen activities are relevant to participants' abilities.
vi) Set a timetable for planning.

Notes
○ Advisers may consult with other appropriate Advisers.
○ For an overnight event, a full programme may not be relevant.

Element 1a

Method of assessment	Signature	Ref no
i)		
ii)		
iii)		
iv)		
v)		
vi)		

Element 1b: select venue and make transport and activity bookings
How do I achieve this?
i) Choose an approved venue, suitable for the type of event chosen.

ii) Consider transport needs.
iii) Ensure plans adhere with Association guidelines by checking *The Guiding Manual*.
iv) Check insurance cover.
v) Book selected venue.
vi) Book activity sessions, as appropriate.
vii) Consider catering requirements.

Note
For an overnight event, there may be few or no catering requirements.

Element 1b

Method of assessment	Signature	Ref no
i)		
ii)		
iii)		
iv)		
v)		
vi)		
vii)		

Element 1c: identify support, taking into consideration experience

How do I achieve this?
i) Identify adult support required.
ii) Identify tasks and roles for participants for the event.
iii) Complete or hold a basic emergency aid or first aid certificate.

Notes
○ Events involving members under the age of 16 must be held within calling distance of an adult who has agreed to help if needed. For expeditions, the adult must be contactable by the group throughout the event and must arrange to meet the group at least once each day.

○ You can attend a Girlguiding UK 1st Response course. Alternatively, St John Ambulance run Young Life Saver and Young Life Saver Plus awards for under-15s and adult courses for those over 15.

Element 1c

Method of assessment	Signature	Ref no
i)		
ii)		
iii)		

Element 1d: communicate and consult with all participants

How do I achieve this?
i) Plan with all participants.
ii) Discuss roles with each member.
iii) Involve everyone when changes are planned.
iv) Prepare and distribute kit list.

Element 1d

Method of assessment	Signature	Ref no
i)		
ii)		
iii)		
iv)		

Module 2
organise and administer a residential event

Element 2a: establish and operate an overall budget

How do I achieve this?
i) Estimate overall costs.
ii) Calculate fees per person based on minimum numbers.
iii) Communicate costs to participants.
iv) Set up an appropriate record for income and expenditure.
v) Collect fees from participants and provide receipts.
vi) Keep receipts and ensure records are accurate and up to date.
vii) Pay bills.
viii) Produce final accounts.

Notes
- Overall costs will include site fees, transport, food, activities, days out, equipment hire, fuel, administration.
- Criteria vii) and viii) may be completed after the event.

Element 2a

Method of assessment	Signature	Ref no
i)		
ii)		
iii)		
iv)		
v)		
vi)		
vii)		
viii)		

Element 2b: decide on equipment
How do I achieve this?
i) Identify and make a list of equipment required for the planned programme.
ii) Find out where to buy/hire/borrow equipment and the cost involved.
iii) Obtain equipment in good time.

Element 2b

Method of assessment	Signature	Ref no
i)		
ii)		
iii)		

Element 2c: complete and distribute Girlguiding UK forms
How do I achieve this?
i) Complete form A/P and have it signed by the Senior Section Leader and, if appropriate, the Guide Leader.
ii) Send form A/P to Commissioner.
iii) Complete and distribute form G/C to participants under 18.
iv) Complete and distribute a health form (G/H) to each participant*.
v) Receive consent slip A/Ac and ensure that it is available throughout the event.
vi) Collect completed form G/C from participants under 18.
vii) Provide final details and explain emergency home contact system to parents/guardians and peers.
viii) Collect each participant's completed health form (G/H) at the beginning of the event and keep safely, but to hand, throughout.

* Once completed, health forms are confidential.

Note
If the person taking the permit is the Senior Section Leader, then the Commissioner should take on the responsibilities of the Leader, as listed in the routing on the reverse of form A/P.

Element 2c

Method of assessment	Signature	Ref no
i)		
ii)		
iii)		
iv)		
v)		
vi)		
vii)		
viii)		

Element 2d: return the facilities in good condition and express thanks

How do I achieve this?

i) Arrange for a final check before leaving.
ii) Ensure the facilities are returned in an acceptable condition to the site owner.
iii) Arrange to thank the adult who was on-call.

Element 2d

Method of assessment	Signature	Ref no
i)		
ii)		
iii)		

LOOK AT **YOURSELF** IN THE WIDER **WORLD.** DO **IT** WITH **LOOK** WIDER.

Module 3
plan for safety and security of self and others

Element 3a: set up and operate emergency procedures
How do I achieve this?
i)   Identify an adult to be the home contact and ensure that they have contact details of participants' parents/guardians.
ii) Establish location of nearest telephone.
iii) Consider any participants with special needs.
iv) Set up emergency procedures for both on and off site.
v)   Brief all participants about emergency procedures.
vi) Demonstrate a knowledge of fire precautions.

Element 3a

Method of assessment	Signature	Ref no
i)		
ii)		
iii)		
iv)		
v)		
vi)		

Element 3b: set ground rules
How do I achieve this?
i)   Ensure that all participants know about emergency procedures to be followed and site rules set by the owner.
ii) Ensure the health and safety of all participants.
iii) Ensure safety of all participants in kitchen areas, including first aid provision.

Note
Criteria iii) does not apply to overnight events with no catering requirements, e.g. when participants eat in cafés and restaurants.

Element 3b

Method of assessment	Signature	Ref no
i)		
ii)		
iii)		

Module 4
organise catering arrangements

Element 4a: establish cooking and storage facilities available

How do I achieve this?
i)   Identify catering and storage facilities.
ii) List catering and storage equipment required.
iii) Obtain necessary equipment.

Element 4a

Method of assessment	Signature	Ref no
i)		
ii)		
iii)		

Element 4b: ensure the planning of a suitable balanced menu

How do I achieve this?
i)   Identify dietary needs of all participants.
ii) Plan menu with participants taking into account programme and time of year.

LOOK AT **YOURSELF** IN **THE** WIDER **WORLD.** DO **IT** WITH **LOOK** WIDER.

iii) Plan menu taking into account cooking methods and storage facilities available.
iv) Plan menu within budget available.
v) List supplies required and organise purchase.
vi) Arrange for the preparation, cooking and serving of food.
vii) Cook at least one hot meal.

Element 4b

Method of assessment　　**Signature**　　**Ref no**

i)

ii)

iii)

iv)

v)

vi)

vii)

Element 4c: set up and maintain good food hygiene standards

How do I achieve this?
i) Set up and maintain hygienic storage facilities.
ii) Establish site requirements for waste disposal.
iii) Make arrangements for waste disposal.

Element 4c

Method of assessment　　**Signature**　　**Ref no**

i)

ii)

iii)

Module 5
make health
and first aid arrangements

Element 5a: establish availability of suitable facilities and utilities
How do I achieve this?
i) Identify safe water supply and ensure provision during the event.
ii) Identify toilet and washing facilities available and maintain standards during the event.

Element 5a
Method of assessment   **Signature**   **Ref no**

i)

ii)

Element 5b: have an up-to-date knowledge of emergency aid and incident management
How do I achieve this?
i) Ensure details of local medical services are available.
ii) Ensure records are kept of all treatment/medication taken.

Note
Each participant should be responsible for administering and keeping safe personal medication. Where possible, medication should be kept locked in a central location.

Element 5b
Method of assessment   **Signature**   **Ref no**

i)

ii)

LOOK AT **YOURSELF** IN **THE** WIDER **WORLD.** DO **IT** WITH **LOOK** WIDER.

Element 5c: check first aid supplies
How do I achieve this?
i) Establish what first aid items are required.
ii) Check existing items are in date.
iii) Purchase necessary supplies.
iv) Ensure first aid kit is available to all during the event.

Note
When cooking facilities are being used, a first aid kit should be kept in the kitchen area.

Element 5c

Method of assessment	Signature	Ref no
i)		
ii)		
iii)		
iv)		

Module 6
organise and maintain equipment for activities

Element 6a: check condition of equipment
How do I achieve this?
i) Prepare list of equipment.
ii) Ensure equipment is checked for safety and suitability before use.
iii) Record any damage as it occurs, and/or defects as they are noticed, and advise owners.

Note
If you can't guarantee that equipment is safe, then seek guidance from an appropriate adult. If someone else,

such as an instructor, is providing equipment she or he should guarantee its safety before it is used and must accept responsibility for its safety.

Element 6a

Method of assessment	Signature	Ref no
i)		
ii)		
iii)		

Element 6b: brief all participants in the care and the safe use of equipment

How do I achieve this?
i) Identify gaps in knowledge of all participants.
ii) Arrange appropriate instruction for equipment to be used in programme activities.
iii) Ensure equipment is cared for and used correctly.
iv) Ensure that hazardous equipment is used and stored safely.

Element 6b

Method of assessment	Signature	Ref no
i)		
ii)		
iii)		
iv)		

Element 6c: arrange for the return of equipment and restocking of consumables

How do I achieve this?
i) Check items against list of equipment.
ii) Ensure all borrowed/hired equipment is returned on time and in good condition.
iii) Replace consumables or organise payment for those used.

LOOK AT **YOURSELF** IN **THE** WIDER **WORLD.** DO **IT** WITH **LOOK** WIDER.

Element 6c

Method of assessment	Signature	Ref no
i)		
ii)		
iii)		

Module 7
organise the care and maintenance of campsite facilities

Element 7a: maintain equipment and facilities for use

How do I achieve this?
i) Decide on the tentage and other equipment.
ii) Brief all participants about the correct use and daily care of equipment and facilities.
iii) Support participants in the care of their personal kit and bedding.

Element 7a

Method of assessment	Signature	Ref no
i)		
ii)		
iii)		

Element 7b: set up camp
How do I achieve this?
i) Lay out the site in a safe and hygienic way.
ii) Pitch the tent(s).
iii) Ensure that the camp has the lowest possible impact on the environment.
iv) Know how to make emergency/small repairs to a tent.
v) Ensure the correct care of tentage for the weather conditions.
vi) Demonstrate safe use of the cooking methods chosen.

Element 7b

Method of assessment	Signature	Ref no
i)		
ii)		
iii)		
iv)		
v)		
vi)		

LOOK AT YOURSELF IN THE WIDER WORLD DO IT WITH LOOK WIDER.

Element 7c: take down equipment and make arrangements for storage

How do I achieve this?
i) Prepare a plan for dismantling the camp.
ii) Allocate tasks to all participants.
iii) Strike the tent(s).
iv) Make arrangements for the cleaning, checking, repairing (as necessary) and packing of equipment.
v) Make contingency plans in the event of wet tents.
vi) Arrange for the storage of equipment.

Element 7c

Method of assessment	Signature	Ref no
i)		
ii)		
iii)		
iv)		
v)		
vi)		

LOOK AT **YOURSELF** IN **THE** WIDER **WORLD.** DO **IT** WITH **LOOK** WIDER.

Module 8

prepare and coordinate a programme of activities for Guides

Element 8a: plan a flexible programme which meets Guides' needs

How do I achieve this?
i) Plan a basic daily programme.
ii) Discuss daily plans with participants.
iii) Determine the time required for each activity.
iv) Review and discuss successes and concerns each day.
v) Plan alternatives for wet weather.

Element 8a

Method of assessment	Signature	Ref no
i)		
ii)		
iii)		
iv)		
v)		

LOOK AT **YOURSELF** IN **THE** WIDER **WORLD.** DO **IT** WITH **LOOK** WIDER.

Module 9
prepare and coordinate an expedition

Element 9a: make preparations, arrangements and carry out

How do I achieve this?

i) Undertake appropriate training or gain a qualification for the chosen method of travel, e.g. walking training scheme, Basic Expedition Leader Award, British Canoe Union award.
ii) Complete a route plan and distribute to relevant Advisers, home contact and adult on-call, where appropriate.
iii) Ensure all participants are capable of the demands of the planned route.
iv) Plan menu and a timetable for purchasing supplies.
v) Ensure that at least one other participant has adequate navigation skills.
vi) Carry out an expedition of at least one night.

Note

Advisers will use the route plan to check that the route is appropriately followed and may meet participants during the event.

Element 9a

Method of assessment	Signature	Ref no
i)		
ii)		
iii)		
iv)		
v)		
vi)		

Module 10
travelling abroad

There is now an additional module for the Senior Section Permit: **Module 10 Travelling abroad**. It was published in the Hotline section of November 2003's *Guiding magazine* and is available on the Senior Section website at www.girlguiding.org.uk/seniorsection

Details of peer group residentials can also be found in the same Hotline, on the website or in *The Guiding Manual 4th Edition*.

If you have any queries about the above, please chat to your Senior Section Adviser or email SeniorSection@girlguiding.org.uk

making it count!

Published by Girlguiding UK
17–19 Buckingham Palace Road
London SW1W 0PT
Email chq@girlguiding.org.uk
Website www.girlguiding.org.uk

Girlguiding UK is an operating name of The Guide Association.
Registered charity number 306016. Incorporated by
Royal Charter.

© The Guide Association 1994-2007

Making It Count! working group: Jean Bell, Jo Chester, Chris Daniels, Sue Dyer, Sarah Gully, Jo Hobbs, Mel Selby
Photographs by Diana Aynaci, Moose Azim, Elizabeth Duffey, Niall Hartley, Kelvin Rogers
Project Editor Rebecca Saraceno
Special Project Designer David Jones
Studio Janie Barton, Jade Garner, Alexandra Valy

Readers are reminded that during the life span of this publication there may be changes to:
○ Girlguiding UK's policy
○ practice or requirements by governing bodies or other organisations
○ legal requirements
which will affect the accuracy of the information contained within these pages.

Contents

About *Making It Count!*	**3**
Me	**7**
Me as a leader	**13**
Leadership in guiding	**21**
Making It Count! contacts	**31**

MAKING IT COUNT! MAKING IT COUNT! **MAKING IT COUNT!** MAKING IT COUNT!

About Making It Count!

Making It Count! is for any member of the Senior Section. It is designed to help you develop leadership skills for personal growth and future projects. Leadership is an essential skill that employers and colleges look out for and so working on *Making It Count!* can really make a difference. Find out how...

As a Guide you may have worked on *Go for It! Teamwork* or done the Team Player or Team Leader interest badges and are looking for the next challenge! You may want to have some recognition of your skills working with younger girls! Or perhaps you want to take up a leadership role and develop skills in preparation for the future! Whatever your desire, you will want to make your experiences and skills count!

How does it work?

Making It Count! gives credit for things you do *in* guiding *and* outside, and encourages you to develop personal and practical skills as well as giving you the chance to gather the knowledge you need. It is arranged in three sections – **Me**, **Me as a leader**, and **Leadership in guiding** – and the challenges have been chosen carefully enabling you to cover many aspects of leadership. You can work on the challenges by yourself or with others in your Senior Section group.

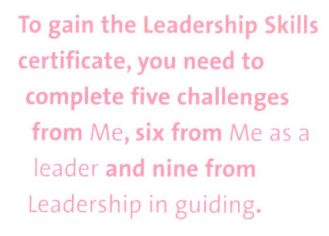

To gain the Leadership Skills certificate, you need to complete five challenges from Me, **six from** Me as a leader **and nine from** Leadership in guiding.

As with your Look Wider challenges, you should discuss your chosen challenges with those in your support group – this may include your Senior Section Leader, the Leader you work with in a unit, and others in your Senior Section group. They will be especially helpful if they too are working on *Making It Count!*. Your support group will help you to decide whether the activity is a real challenge for you and will discuss your achievements with you when you are ready (see page 13 in your *Look Wider* personal organiser or page 52 of the *Look Wider* file).

Before you start

It is a very good idea to consider whether you would like to count a challenge for both *Making It Count!* and Look Wider, and if so, you must plan to do so in advance and agree it with your support group. Before you get into working on your challenges, take a look at the 'Making contact' pages in the *Look Wider* file (pages 71–104). This is full of useful information to help you plan and carry out your chosen activities.

Once you have completed all the challenges you should discuss your achievements with your support group who will confirm them and help you to celebrate! You will also want to decide on a suitable event for presentation of your Leadership Skills certificate!

At 16 you can start working towards the Leadership Qualification. A lot of what you do for *Making It Count!* can be used for this qualification, so make sure you record everything you do. When you start the Leadership Qualification you will be assigned a mentor. Make sure you show her your records from *Making It Count!* and discuss how anything you have done can be accredited across.

Use the 'my challenge' boxes on the following pages to record what you have done for each of the challenges. Don't forget that you should evaluate everything that you do. For a quick review of every challenge, simply tick the appropriate symbol giving it a thumbs-up, thumbs-down or not-so-sure. There's also some space to record people with whom you have come into contact during *Making It Count!*. These people could be useful to know in the future, so try to build up relationships with them.

Where am I?

Use the checklist on the next page to find out how your skills are as a leader and which areas you need to work on. If you are feeling really brave you could ask your Leader to fill it in as well, then compare your results with hers. The checklist has been divided into three time periods so as you progress through *Making It Count!* you can see your development growing. Remember to come back at the half way period and then finally at the end to add to your record.

Yes, I can do that

Sometimes, but not enough

Not really, I need to work on that

Mark which symbol best describes you at the start of working on *Making it Count!*, at the half way point and then finally at the end.

	Start	Half way	Finish
I listen to what other people say	👎 👊 👍	👎 👊 👍	👎 👊 👍
I am ready to try new ideas	👎 👊 👍	👎 👊 👍	👎 👊 👍
I learn new skills on my own	👎 👊 👍	👎 👊 👍	👎 👊 👍
I manage my time so that I can get everything done	👎 👊 👍	👎 👊 👍	👎 👊 👍
I know where to ask for help if I need it	👎 👊 👍	👎 👊 👍	👎 👊 👍
I am sufficiently confident to share my skills with others	👎 👊 👍	👎 👊 👍	👎 👊 👍
I can set goals for myself	👎 👊 👍	👎 👊 👍	👎 👊 👍
I contribute ideas thoughtfully and tactfully	👎 👊 👍	👎 👊 👍	👎 👊 👍
I don't mind criticism and try to use it	👎 👊 👍	👎 👊 👍	👎 👊 👍
I have a sense of humour and know when to use it	👎 👊 👍	👎 👊 👍	👎 👊 👍
I can come up with solutions to problems and work to achieve them	👎 👊 👍	👎 👊 👍	👎 👊 👍
I can see other people's points of view	👎 👊 👍	👎 👊 👍	👎 👊 👍
I can talk to a group of people I do not know very well	👎 👊 👍	👎 👊 👍	👎 👊 👍
I can learn from what I have done	👎 👊 👍	👎 👊 👍	👎 👊 👍
I can control my moods	👎 👊 👍	👎 👊 👍	👎 👊 👍

MAKING IT COUNT! MAKING IT COUNT! **MAKING IT COUNT!** MAKING IT COUNT!

Me

Me is all about yourself, helping you to find out what you are good at, and to build on your strengths. Working through this section will help you to identify and develop skills and attitudes that will be useful throughout your life.

Complete one challenge under each of the following headings, you may do more if you wish.

Communication

Pick five favourite songs and look at the message they put across. Is it the words or the music that conveys the message? How is this done? Explain to your support group why these five are your favourites.

Find out your communication style by doing the exercise on pages 21–24 of your *Look Wider* personal organiser. Decide how can you use the results of this activity to help you in the future.

Pick a challenge from the 'Word play' section of the Creativity Octant (*Look Wider*, page 17).

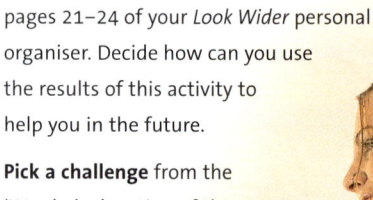

My challenge

My values

Draw a time map and mark on it the important events in your life. Project your time map into the future as far as you can. How do you see your life developing? What sort of choices and decisions will you have to make? Are there any events in your time map so far that may help you with these choices?

Many times in life you can be faced with a choice between doing what you think is right or being one of the crowd. Plan a play, sketch or story to illustrate these choices and share it with your peer group. Think about issues like bullying, assertiveness and breaking the law. Your play, sketch or story should consider the consequences of the choices you can make.

Pick a challenge from the 'Who am I?' section in the Personal values Octant (*Look Wider*, pages 40–41).

My challenge

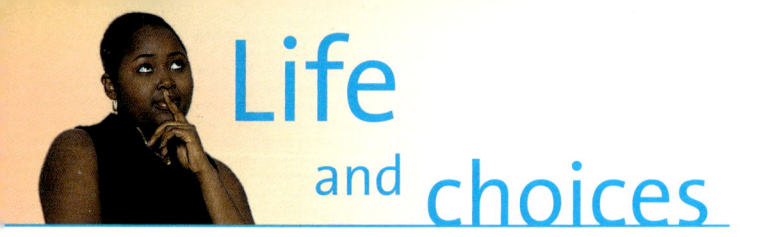

Life and choices

How do some people cram so much into their lives? School, homework, going out, TV and guiding all take up so much time. Work out how you use your time over a week (a chart may help) and discuss it with your peers. Count all 24 hours of each day – remember to include eating and sleeping! How much spare time do you have to do those things you never find time to do?

Do you know what age you can legally work part-time and for how many hours? Find out the minimum legal age for the items in the list below and think about how this affects you and the way you live your life. Share your thoughts with your peers. ○ See different categories of film? ○ Vote in elections? ○ Have a passport? ○ Open a bank account? ○ Go to a pet shop and buy a pet? ○ Join the armed forces? ○ Get married with your parents' consent? ○ Go into a pub? ○ Buy a drink in a pub? ○ Leave home?

Pick a challenge from the 'Social structures' section in the Independent living Octant (*Look Wider*, page 36).

My challenge

Understanding others

Find out about a religion or faith that is different to your own, and visit a place of worship or talk to someone who believes in the faith you have chosen.

Share with your Senior Section group what you have found out about a culture that is different from your own. Compare different aspects of your lifestyles. What is similar?

Pick a challenge from the 'Alternative lives' section in the International Octant (*Look Wider*, page 35).

My challenge

Developing your skills

What's your learning style? Complete the activity on pages 19–20 of your *Look Wider* personal organiser and see how this applies to you. Are you surprised by the result? How can you apply this to your future learning needs?

Pick a challenge from the 'Life supports' section in the Independent living Octant (*Look Wider*, page 39).

My challenge

Me as a leader

Me as a leader encourages you to arrange activities both by yourself and with others. It looks at personal and practical skills as well as the knowledge that leaders need. Remember that in this section, the group you choose to work with can be from any area of your life, for example at school or through a hobby, and not just in guiding.

Complete one challenge under each of the following headings, you may do more if you wish.

Communication

Choose a fun game, teaching game, and testing game. Try them out on your group. Compare how differently you need to handle each type of game. Does one type of game work better with your group? Why do you think this is? Try using the planning and evaluation sheets on pages 109–110 of the *Look Wider* file to help you, and discuss what you have learnt with the group's leader.

Hold a 'balloon debate'. Your group is in a hot-air balloon that is running out of helium and will crash within a certain time. There's only one parachute on board so only one person can be saved. Each adopt a role, e.g. pop star, doctor or a mother caring for children, and argue convincingly for salvation. When the time runs out, collectively decide who uses the parachute.

Watch a selection of soap operas and identify situations where communication breaks down. Think about how communication works. Explain what you have seen to someone in your support group.

My challenge

Understanding others

Organise and carry out activities that make you think about physical disabilities. For example, lead a blindfolded person around the building or learn some basic sign language. Ask your group what they have learned about others' lives.

Find out if there are any special needs groups in your area and make arrangements to visit one. Discuss with their leaders whether the leadership skills that are required in this situation are very different.

Pick a challenge from the 'Dealing with disability' section in the Independent living Octant (*Look Wider*, pages 37–38).

My challenge

ME AS A LEADER ME AS A LEADER **ME AS A LEADER** ME AS A LEADER **ME AS A LEADER**

Presentation

Show someone how to do something that you are already good at. Try to remember what helped you to learn to do the activity well, and make a mental note of it so that you can pass on and try out any useful tips.

Present your view on any topic to a small group. Use methods such as posters, photographs, videotape or a cassette tape. As part of your preparation observe the styles of presenters on different media such as television and radio.

Tell a story to a group of people. You could tell a story about an activity you have done, or one about the history of guiding. You could choose a story that is meant to be read aloud.

My challenge

Leadership skills

Find out about 4ward, 4self, 4others which is a peer education initiative. Invite a local In4mer along to your group meeting to share some of their skills. How does peer education work and why?

List all the skills you think a good leader needs. Explain to your support group which are the four most important and why.

Pick a challenge from the 'Swot up on your skills' section in the Leadership Octant (*Look Wider*, pages 44–46).

My challenge

Safety first

Know the appropriate emergency or safety precautions for your meeting place – such as where the nearest exits and extinguishers are, how to stack tables and chairs safely.

Know the contents of and how to use the first aid kit in the place where you hold your meetings.

My challenge

ME AS A LEADER ME AS A LEADER **ME AS A LEADER** ME AS A LEADER **ME AS A LEADER**

Running the finances

Help plan and carry out an activity to raise money with the group you are working with, or with your Senior Section group. Remember that you need to raise enough money to cover your expenses, and keep a record of the accounts.

Plan the budget for a special event for your school, club or unit, such as a day out. Find out how much money you can use from funds, and how much will have to be paid by the individuals attending the event. Make sure you account for all costs, including transport, food and equipment.

Help the treasurer with the unit accounts for a term.

My challenge

ME AS A LEADER ME AS A LEADER ME AS A LEADER ME AS A LEADER ME AS A LEADER

MAKING IT COUNT! MAKING IT COUNT! **MAKING IT COUNT!** MAKING IT COUNT!

Leadership in guiding

Leadership in guiding focuses on using the skills you have developed in guiding, perhaps as a Young Leader or helping at other guiding events locally.

Complete one challenge under each of the following headings. You may do more if you wish.

Communication

Find out how local guiding communication channels work. Go to your District meetings and any other meetings you are able to attend to find out what is going on.

How does your unit pass on all the information that is needed to the members' parents? With the help of your Unit Leader, make sure all the necessary information is given to parents for an event. How effective was it? Could other methods be used?

Choose a challenge from the 'Send out a clear message' section in the Leadership Octant (*Look Wider*, page 49).

My challenge

Presentation

Keep a record of a term's activities in the unit you are working with. This could be in any form such as a scrapbook, a diary or cassette recordings.

Design a leaflet or poster to promote an event or guiding in general to an external audience. Use the 'Shout about it!' section on pages 113–122 of *Look Wider* for some help.

Put together a display on any aspect of guiding for the unit you are working with. Make sure it is suitable for the age group and gives as much information as is needed.

My challenge

LEADERSHIP IN GUIDING LEADERSHIP IN GUIDING **LEADERSHIP IN GUIDING** LEADERSHIP

Understanding others

Talk with the Leader from the unit you are working with and find out about how the needs of individual girls can be met. For example, discuss how you could support the exceptionally able girl, one who is very shy or a member of your unit who has a broken leg.

Follow the progress of a particular girl over several weeks and help her to achieve success in something she finds difficult. Explain what you have done to your support group.

Help a Brownie or Guide choose and carry out a challenge, or help a Rainbow achieve something she has difficulties with. You could help her to look in the section's resources for some ideas.

My challenge

Programme

Discuss with your Unit Leader how she ensures that the unit's programme is well-balanced, and why a balanced programme is important. Take a part in planning a term's programme.

Take part in a Rainbow Chat, Brownie Pow-wow or Patrol Leaders' Council. Explain to your support group why it is important to listen to the members of the unit when planning the programme.

Find out about the Five Essentials. Discuss with the Unit Leader how they can all be incorporated into the programme.

Familiarise yourself with Girlguiding UK publications for the section you are working with and use them to plan and carry out a unit meeting on a theme.

My challenge

Working with others

Work with others outside your unit's leadership team to plan an activity. This could be a Rainbow picnic, Brownie out of unit experience or a Guide fun day.

Participate, with others from your unit or people who are new to you, in some team-building activities. Look at some of the publications for ideas and try one with girls in your unit.

Pick a challenge from the 'Engage with others' section in the Leadership Octant (*Look Wider*, pages 46–47).

My challenge

Organising activities

Choose an idea for a game or activity and adapt it so that it is suitable for a different age group. For example, alter a game or activity for Rainbows so that Brownies would find it challenging. When you have worked out your idea, either give it a go with your group, or ask a Leader to try it out.

Organise a wide game for your unit.

Pick a challenge from the 'Make things happen' section in the Leadership Octant (*Look Wider*, page 47).

My challenge

The Promise

Create and use an activity to help a group of girls in your unit understand the Promise and Law.

Take a full part in discussing and organising a Promise ceremony. Make sure the person or people who are taking their Promise are involved in all ideas and planning.

Discuss with an adult member of your choice the understanding you have of the Promise, and how it helps you in your leadership role in your unit.

My challenge

Guiding around the world

Create and use an activity to help girls in your unit learn about World Thinking Day.

Find out about the Guide Friendship Fund and any projects that it is currently funding. Plan and carry out an activity with your unit to raise some money for it.

Choose an activity from *A World of Ideas* or *Friends Round the World* or *Explore-A-Pack* and use it to help girls know and understand more about other cultures and people.

Pick a challenge from the 'Cultural exchange' section in the International Octant (*Look Wider*, page 34).

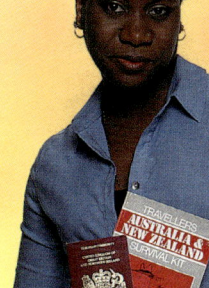

My challenge

LEADERSHIP IN GUIDING LEADERSHIP IN GUIDING **LEADERSHIP IN GUIDING** LEADERSHIP   29

Out and about

Share in the organisation of and take part in a Rainbow ramble, Brownie Holiday, Brownie out of unit experience, Guide camp, Guide holiday or an expedition for members of the Senior Section.

Make a nature trail or leave a trail of clues for a group to follow which allows them to explore an area, or to discover something, or to find ingredients for their meal.

Find an activity in the Out of doors Octant (*Look Wider*, pages 28–31) that you can carry out with your unit. Make all the necessary preparations, including suitable safety arrangements, and carry out the activity.

My challenge

LEADERSHIP IN GUIDING LEADERSHIP IN GUIDING **LEADERSHIP IN GUIDING** LEADERSHIP

Making It Count!
contacts

- Name
- Address
- Postcode
- ☎
- Mobile
- Email

- Name
- Address
- Postcode
- ☎
- Mobile
- Email

Making It Count!
contacts

Name
Address

Postcode
( )
Mobile
E-mail

Name
Address

Postcode
( )
Mobile
E-mail

Making It Count! is for any member of the Senior Section – although primarily aimed at 14–16 year olds. It is especially designed to help you develop vital leadership skills which are essential for personal growth and future projects. Find out how working on *Making It Count!* can really make a difference...

Girlguiding UK